Moses spends much of his time touring ...etry and percussion show around the schools, libraries and festivals.

...cat called Elvis actually did move into ...village, next door to where Brian lives, ...d provided the inspiration for two poems.

Sadly Elvis is no more, and although Brian's dog's plans to eliminate Elvis were at an advanced stage, she did, after all, have nothing to do with the manner of his passing. Rock on Elvis, wherever you are!

Contact Brian via his website:
www.brianmoses.co.uk

Raised by ninjas in the barren wastes of West Yorkshire, **Chris Garbutt** was trained in the mystical art of scribbling and doodling.

He currently drives a motorized cheeseburger around the sunny streets of Southern California, fuelled by nothing but tea and biscuits.

Other books by Brian Moses

(100% Unofficial) Olympic Poems
Brian Moses and Roger Stevens

Greetings, Earthlings!
Space poems by Brian Moses and James Carter

The Truth About Parents
*Hilarious rhymes by Paul Cookson,
David Harmer, Brian Moses and Roger Stevens*

A Cat Called ELVIS

Brilliant Poems by BRIAN MOSES

Illustrated by Chris Garbutt

MACMILLAN CHILDREN'S BOOKS

First published 2012 by Macmillan Children's Books
a division of Macmillan Publishers Limited
20 New Wharf Road, London N1 9RR
Basingstoke and Oxford
Associated companies throughout the world
www.panmacmillan.com

ISBN 978-0-230-75197-2

1 3 5 7 9 8 6 4 2

A CIP catalogue record for this book is available from
the British Library.

Printed and bound by CPI Group (UK) Ltd, Croydon CR0 4YY

Contents

Targets

My teacher says my targets are:

To write more neatly,
to spell more words correctly,
to get more sums right,
to chatter less
and to behave myself.

But the targets I set myself
are far more interesting:

To climb a tree to the top,
to stop time before my spelling test,
to think up a disappearing spell
and try it out on my
    teacher,
to leap from up high
and to defy gravity.

These are my targets,
the ones I'm aiming to
    complete
before next week . . .

The ones my teacher sets
may take a little longer . . .

Hercules' Gym

Eros, the god of love,
and Ares, the god of war,
are often to be seen
in combat on the floor,

wrestling, one with the other,
each one hoping to win,
but war will never surrender
and love will never give in,

down at Hercules' gym,
we're training
down at Hercules' gym.

And Atlas, statue still,
will advise you on lifting weights,
instructing you how to spin
a pile of tectonic plates.

And then he'll test your strength,
watching you juggle with boulders
till finally you're ready to take
the weight of the world on your shoulders,

down at Hercules' gym,
we're training
down at Hercules' gym.

And you'll meet your fitness trainer,
a shifty guy called Hades,
who thinks he's Mr Universe
and flatters all the ladies.

But if you make Hades mad
you'll wonder what's got into him
as a swift punch breaks your jaw
and all your lights go dim,

down at Hercules' gym,
we're training
down at Hercules' gym.

And it's best to pretend
you haven't seen
Medusa on
the rowing machine.

Just turn right round
and leave for home
unless you fancy
being set in stone

down at Hercules' gym,
everybody's going
down to Hercules' gym.

So visit today, get real,
get a special promotional deal,

down at Hercules' gym,
down at Hercules' gym,
down at Hercules' gym.

(Just tell 'em,
Zeus sent you.)

A Cat Called Elvis

(A cat called Elvis moved in next door . . .)

Elvis is Elvis before he joined the army.

No Vegas cat, fat and fortuned,
he's lean and mean,
a sneer on his face.

Kills birds,
knocks 'em dead.

A cat to be scared of,
a twist of the hip,
a curl of the lip.

No diplomat,
he's a rock 'n' roll cat.

A cat on the wall,
caterwauling.

Bad news for any dog
who steps on his
blue suede shoes!

Skunk Attack

(In America, if your dog gets skunked you cannot bear to have him in the house. He has to live in the backyard for up to a year. It is one of the worst smells imaginable.)

Don't drop bombs on anyone,
drop skunks . . .

Skunk spray smell won't disappear,
it's the odour all dog owners fear.

It's worse than a machine gun's *ack-ack-ack*
when your choice of weapon is a skunk attack.

When Sergeant Major Skunk knocks on your
   door
then rumbles his way across the floor,

you can roll into a ball, you can get down low,
but there really is no place for you to go.

A skunk paratrooper knows just what to do
and he's going to make such a mess out of you.

For when he's done spraying, everyone will fear
   you.
Even your Mama won't want to come near you.

Your brothers and sisters will say goodbye.
You'll be locked in a room till a year goes by.

There's no perfume that you could spray
to take the stink of skunk away.

It's the sort of smell that drives you insane,
it gets worse with water, worse in the rain.

So what will you do about skunk paratroopers
that twist and turn like hula hoopers

as they drop from the sky? Well, you'd better
    run.
Don't drop bombs on anyone,

Drop skunks.

*(Thanks for the
idea, Flick.)*

Doesn't Mix with Cats
(*Sign on the door of a dog kennel*)

I ain't no la-di-da dog
who cuddles up to a cat.
You won't find any cat space
upon my welcome mat.

Cats have been there for chasing
right down through history.
How any dog can make friends with one
is one huge mystery.

We've never made peace with cats,
it's always been out and out war,
dogs have always fought cats,
it's always been tooth and claw.

A dog just needs his space,
not some in-your-face sort of cat
who climbs into bed beside him
or snuggles close on the mat.

Share with one cat today
and you'll share with others tomorrow.
It's dumb making peace with cats,
it can only bring you sorrow.

One minute you'll be relaxing,
stretched out, warming your paws,
then you'll hear the click of the cat flap
and in slinks the cat from next door.

So you growl and you snarl and you bark
and you do what all dogs should do,
but there really is no justice at all
when the one that gets thrown out is you!

My Dog

My dog doesn't need watches,
my dog doesn't need clocks.
My dog doesn't need hoodies,
leather jackets or socks.

My dog doesn't need lattes,
my dog doesn't need tea.
My dog doesn't need the Internet,
or a villa in Italy.

My dog doesn't need politics,
my dog doesn't need religion.
My dog doesn't need radio
or a flat-screen television.

My dog doesn't need books,
my dog doesn't need school.
My dog doesn't need money
or other dogs saying she's cool!

My dog doesn't need a holiday
to some exotic place.
My dog doesn't need make-up
spread across her face.

My dog doesn't need mobile phones
ringing her constantly.
My dog doesn't need technology,
my dog just needs me,

the hills, the woods, the fields,
the rivers and the streams.
And a rabbit to chase now and then,
both in and out of her dreams.

A Book of Smells

Wouldn't it be good
to write a book
that dogs could read?

Not a book with words,
the kind of words that weave spells
through the reader's mind,
but instead
a book of smells.

Dogs could sniff their way
through a book
as each new page
brings a different aroma,
each fresh smell
a new jolt to the nose.

From the dropped pizza
and brimming bins
of city alleyways
to countryside cows
and sheep.

The smell of rabbits
would get them leaping
from one page
to the next.

The smell of
  pies cooking
would get them
drooling.

To smell a rat
would get them
  racing.

Rich smells of
  perfumes
and caviar
would entice
celebrity dogs
from their
  cushions.

What a whole new dawn
for dogs,
what stimulation
from new sensations.

For Honey and Bumble,
for Buster and Nelson,
a book of smells
would quickly become
a best
        s(m)eller!

New York Dogs

New York dogs get everywhere,
in doggy playgroups on Washington Square.
Peeping out of handbags, cool and chic,
in bookshop windows, fast asleep.
In a hobo's shopping cart after dark,
jogging with the runners through Central Park.
Waiting at the lights for the 'Walk, don't walk',
yawning while their owners talk the talk.
One with bootees to keep paws clean,
one with a big guy, both looking mean.
One clip-clopping, huge as a horse,
one leaning out the window of a Porsche.
One wearing shades around Times Square,
New York dogs get everywhere.

A Wolf Is Howling Still

In trim suburban gardens
or pacing the streets of town,
somewhere a wolf is still howling,
somewhere a wolf is still around.

In the hustle and bustle of cities
where tower blocks reach for the sky,
somewhere a wolf is still howling
his dark primeval cry.

It's not something you always hear,
you need to tune yourself in,
latch on to a primitive wavelength
beneath the urban skin.

It will bring back the lost and the left behind
that we thought disappeared forever.
The wolf that never went away,
the wolf that was far too clever.

It's there, below the streets,
in the distance, high on a hill.
Caught on the web of the breeze
a wolf is howling still.

You need to learn to listen,
it's a message, an ancient clue.
Somewhere a wolf is still howling
and it may be calling to you.

Walking Dogs, Christmas Day
(*Yorkshire Moors, 2009*)

One dog guides us through the fields
on a route she's followed for years.
No matter the track has disappeared
under layers of snow, old-timer Charlie
still knows which way to go.

Fern just wants to play, to bullet herself
through drifting snow. Six months old,
she's never seen the fields white out
like this before. Suddenly her world becomes
a wet and wacky playground she can't ignore.

Lucy wants to confide in us.
She knows this place, has seen it change,
summer gold to winter white.
She holds us spellbound, hints at secrets
only dogs discover, closer to the ground.

Bruno cracks us up, part dachshund,
part terrier, long narrow face
like Uncle Bulgaria, barely bigger
than the depth of snow, squeezes his shape,
cartoon-like, into spaces he shouldn't go.

But Scampi stays at home, snug in her own
small hiding hole. Nothing we say
can persuade her to come, the snow too deep,
the ice too cold. She'll hibernate
till old bones feel a warmer season unfold.

Our Dog's Tail

Christmas trees guaranteed non-drop
just can't withstand the flip
and flop of our dog's tail.

Our dog's tail should be listed
in *The Guinness Book*
for speed, velocity
and sheer tail power.

Our dog could generate electricity.
Keep her happy, and her wagging tail
could set light bulbs burning
for hours and hours.

Our dog's tail could conduct symphonies.
A bright and upbeat movement
in praise of walking the hills,
a mad, fast part
when she's squirrel-chasing,
a slow and lazy andante
for sleeping in the sun.

She could easily be
a cheerleader,
or flag-waver.

If only we could harness
our dog's tail,
make use of
one small part of her ...

but even when we call her
'Useless Lump',
we still hear her
beating time on the floor,
the thump, thump, thump
of our dog's tail
giving rhythm
to our day.

Guilty

Honey is most certainly guilty,
it's written all over her face.
Whatever it is, the dog did it,
the dog is in disgrace.

Honey is looking sorrowful,
there's that hangdog look in her eyes.
She can't do innocent when guilty,
she's incapable of telling lies.

She knows that we're usually angry,
that we'll rant and rage for a bit,
or storm about and send her out
and that'll be the end of it.

But this time the dog went too far
and chewed up a twenty-pound note.
Dad pulled from her mouth what was left of it
while the rest disappeared down her throat.

Now Dad calls her all sorts of names
and then rages and rants some more,
while she hides beneath the table
and looks mournfully down at the floor.

And Honey won't be his honey
until his annoyance has passed,
then she knows she'll be forgiven,
she knows that his anger won't last.

Tomorrow Dad's heart will soften,
the dog will be cuddled again.
He'll rub her tummy, then roll on the floor
and act like he's nine or ten.

But for now an uncrossable void
exists between dog and Dad,
while Honey's already forgotten
what she did that made Dad mad.

Space Dog

She must have been someone's pet,
sometime before the scientists
found her, tagged and labelled her
suitable for space.
She had, someone said,
a trusting face.

She must have been shocked
when the ones she'd trusted
strapped her down
in some strange contraption,
stroked her head, tickled
under her chin, then left
and locked her in.

She must have been cowed
by the rocket's power,
shaken by the roar, the thrust
must have left her
shivering, with no one there
to calm her down
when she needed it most.

She must have whined
for a long time, while wires
taped to her skin
relayed her reactions.

She must have thought
it was some sort of game
gone painfully wrong
and that very soon they'd
release her.

She must have closed her eyes
when the temperature rose.
I hope she was thinking of trees,
of running through fields.

And if only they'd had the means
to bring her back,
she would have given them
her usual welcome,
forgiven them too,
like dogs forgive all humans
the hurtful things they do.

Dead Dinosaurs

One hundred and sixty-five million years
    the dinosaur dynasty lasted,
till solar flares or some meteor
    meant dinosaurs got blasted,
knocked off their feet, burned to black,
    or drowned by an angry sea.
And since that day, great dinosaurs
    have just been history.

And they stamped their footprints into the soil
    to let us know they'd been around.
And they left their mark on this planet,
    we found their bones in the ground.
In the strata and substrata
    we found their teeth and claws,
we found their tails and vertebrae,
    we found their massive jaws.

And we felt the ground start shaking
And we heard deep distant roars.
Then we knew we'd had a message
from dead dinosaurs.

These dinosaurs are telling us
    what we don't want to believe.
They're telling us that very soon
    we'll be the ones to leave.
It seems we're just a footnote,
    the last line of a page,

but look at the damage we've done
in our technological age.

And this time will be for good,
there won't be any return.
This planet will be a desert
where everything will burn.
Till highly evolved space creatures
discover our world some day,
then shake their heads and wonder
why we let it get this way.

And they'll feel the ground start shaking
And they'll hear deep distant roars
And they'll know they've got a message
from dead dinosaurs,
from dead dinosaurs.

Empty Places

I like empty places.

The woods, the stream, the fields.

It's knowing I've no need
to make connections with anyone
about anything.

It's knowing I don't have to speak,
and that no one can contact me.

And the places themselves
are secure in their silence.
The landscape keeps tight-lipped,
it has no wish to reveal
its secrets.

(Although, just occasionally
I detect the whisperings of leaves,
the gossip of greenery.)

There are times of course
when my fingers feel the pulse of the city,
when its heartbeat connects with mine.
There are times too
when I need to be vocal,
when I need to crack the surface of silence.

But then it's back to those empty places,
that desire to be somewhere where no one else
    is,
to feel, to touch, to surf the breeze.

I like empty places,
the woods, the stream, the fields,
those kinds of places
that I can fill
with my dreams.

City Dragons

There must be dragons beneath
the manhole covers on New York streets.
How else to explain the random gusts
of steam that curl round your feet.
How else to explain the distant roar
from tunnels beneath the ground,
or the rain-washed streets at night
that make a hissing sound.

I warn you stay clear of darkness,
keep your feet on the sunny side,
don't seek out underworld shadows
where all the crazies hide.
It's a parallel world you'll find there,
one that you won't want to share,
don't make it easy for dragons below
to pull you down to their lair.

And don't walk over gratings,
they could trip you, send you stumbling,
hidden trapdoors could reveal themselves,
give way and send you tumbling
down and down to this other world,
this world of the almost dead.
Be wise, steer clear and always keep
the stars above your head.

For this underworld is another world
existing under your feet,
and there really is something down there
that you wouldn't want to meet.
There's a huffing and a puffing
of a dragon's city breath,
and a claw reaching up from a grating
to pull you down to your death.

Dragon Path

*(For Crowhurst village school, who gave this
name to a path in their playground)*

Nothing will be the same as before
once you've drawn a dragon to your door,
once a dragon knows just where to find you
you'll always have to look behind you,
always have to take great care
once you summon a dragon from its lair.
And it won't be any kind of joke
if you see flames, if you smell smoke
or wake to find in dread of night,
half the village set alight.
Then next day finding your head teacher
protecting the school from this fearful creature,
flameproofing the roof, soundproofing the doors
to block out the noise of its dragony roars.
While you're inside, preparing for SATS,
the dragon is feasting on barbecued cats.
Avoiding the dragon will drive you insane.
I suggest you rename your path 'Sweet Hamster
   Lane'.

Valentine

The blueberry in your muffin,
the froth on top of your coffee,
the toothpaste on your toothbrush,
that's what I'd like to be.

The dirt beneath your fingernails,
the earwax in your ear,
the ketchup stain on your shirt
that just won't disappear.

The only tune on your iPod,
that's what I'd like to be.
The smile that captures your face
whenever you think of me . . . (I wish . . .)

A dust particle in your jumper,
a string on your guitar,
the shoelace in your shoe,
the steering wheel of your car.

If only I could be with you
I'd willingly do any task.
Say that you'll be mine,
it isn't a lot to ask.

The Dragons Are Hiding

To be born a dragon hunter
is somehow to know that, once,
a very long time ago, dragons
were not just the stuff of dreams.
It was a way for young men
to fulfil their destinies, to ride off
on horseback, seeking treasure.
It was, first and foremost,
a measure of their courage,
the best sort of quest.

It was a solitary pursuit, one to one,
hunter and hunted, the odds even.
Sharp eyes, cunning and surprise
all counted, for a lick of flame
would be all it took to paralyse.
Dragons knew they were young men's
quarry, they became elusive, led
secluded lives, slept by day, fed
at night, easily fled when challenged.

Then down the years, dragons
disappeared. There were tales
of course, a mountain in Scotland,
a labyrinth in Wales, but the trails
proved cold: no smoke-blackened
caves, no burned-out villages,
no graves of would-be dragon
hunters.

Yet recently there were rumours again:
the whisper of wing-beats in darkness,
distant thunder from mountains,
a tumult beneath a waterfall, where roaring
could easily be disguised.

Any young warrior out seeking dragons
should look again, in slate caverns
and abandoned mineshafts.
They should travel to the hidden sides
of mountains, look beneath devils'
bridges and daringly dig
to discover the silent secret spaces
where dragons might be waking.

For in a darkening Welsh landscape
with evening purpling the hills,
it is easy, so easy to believe
how those of us who would be
dragon hunters, could one day
find them again.

(Written near Machynlleth, pronounced
MA HUCH HUN TH LETH)

Spider-swallowing

This may be something you do not know,
indeed it may be something you do not wish to
    know,
but you are, almost certainly,
a spider swallower.

You don't know it's happening,
but be assured it does.

It's easy to swallow mozzies or midges or flies.
You open your mouth to shout out something
    to your mates
and then before you know it.
something takes a nosedive
down the black hole of your throat.

But spider-swallowing happens at night.

Fast asleep, you're on your back, mouth open,
when a spider that's been happily exploring
　　your ceiling
suddenly sees your face from above and lets
　　down a line.

Seeing the open trapdoor of your mouth, it
　　thinks,
I'll just slip inside.

And at that moment, when you feel something
　　tickle your teeth,
your mouth snaps shut.

Then there's only one place for the spider to
　　hide,
so it carries on down into your insides,
never to be seen again.

When you wake next morning you don't
　　remember a thing,
but the fact is, **everyone swallows at least
eight spiders in one lifetime!**

Air Guitar

I'm hoping I might get some recognition
if I win the air-guitar competition.

I've got the most brilliant air guitar,
I found it on eBay, it'll make me a star.

And it's simple, there's really nothing to it,
in fact any fool can be sure to do it.

This instrument never gives me sore fingers,
it's always in tune when I play.
I never hit any wrong notes,
it's in perfect pitch every day.

Some days it's a Fender,
some days a Telecaster.
Some days it's a Rickenbacker
or a twin-necked Stratocaster.

And some days, yes, I'm Clapton,
Jimi Hendrix or Kurt Cobain,
or that guy in a spandex suit,
I just can't remember his name!

And I'm playing the guitar behind my back,
I'm playing it with my teeth,
I'm playing it upside down, back to front
and underneath.

And I can make it *whine*,
I can make it *growl*,
I can make it *hum*,
and I can make it *howl* . . .

I can play it really loud,
I can play it soft and low,
I can play it so breakneck fast
that my fingers seem to glow.

And I know that every one of you
would like to play like me.
Just hold your invisible axe,
now, are you ready, 1-2-3 . . .

Reasons Why I Don't Play Air Guitar Any More

1. My best friend borrowed it and never gave it back.

2. I left it on a train and now British Rail claims they can't find it.

3. My dad said it made too much noise and confiscated it till I learn to play properly. (But how can I learn to play properly if I can't practise?)

4. I lost the instruction manual.

5. Mum said she thought it was broken and put it out for the binmen.

6. Every time I played it my dog started howling.

7. Dad sat on it and now the neck's broken.

8. Every time I picked it up I got an electric shock.

9. It produced such terrible feedback.

10. It needs new strings.

Anyway, everyone plays air guitar these days. I've just ordered an air keyboard – from eBay of course!

Space Station 215

This is Space Station 215
letting you know that we're still alive
and kicking, out here at Planet Rock
with DJ Robot, your cosmic jock.

We're bringing you these sounds from space,
sounds that will take you to some other place.
We got Androids, Humanoids, Starlighters
    too,
we got Moondog and Big Star, just for you.

We got a shipload of sounds comin' in today,
flying them fast along the Milky Way.
We got R & B, we got rock 'n' roll,
we got the strangest sounds from a deep black
    hole.

We got Mercury Rev, we got Moontrekkers
    too,
we got Sigue Sigue Sputnik comin' to you.
We got all sorts of music to give you a lift,
we're rockin' so hard we'll make your planet
    shift.

So listen in and listen good
to these sounds we bring to your
    neighbourhood.
Just turn your radio up to the sky,
we're blasting down from way up high.

This is Space Station 215
letting you know that we're still alive
and kicking, out here at Planet Rock
with DJ Robot, your cosmic jock.

Rocket-watching Party

(Jaycee Beach was the nearest beach to Cape Canaveral – later renamed Cape Kennedy – where rockets were launched. In the 1950s there were regular rocket-watching parties along the beach.)

There's a rocket-watching party
at the beach tonight
and we'll cheer the rocket
till it's way out of sight.

Bring something to eat,
bring burgers and Coke,
bring binoculars
for the first sign of smoke.

We'll pick up driftwood
from along the shore,
build up a fire
as we wait for the roar,

for the whoosh of flame
that grows higher and higher
reaching to the heavens
in a trail of fire.

And we'll tremble with excitement
or maybe fear
as it blusters skywards
then disappears.

And all of us want to be
rocket engineers,
pilots or scientists,
space pioneers.

But sometimes we wait
and we wait and wait
and nothing happens
and it's getting late.

Till a message comes through,
no launch tonight,
countdown's called off
it just didn't go right.

Then it's just another night
on Jaycee Beach
when the stars still seem
so far out of reach.

A Fish Ventriloquist

I wanted to be the world's first fish ventriloquist,
so I searched and searched for the sort of fish
that might share the spotlight with me,
till somewhere near the Caspian Sea
I spoke with a cod who had found God,
but all he wanted to do was pray with me.
In Yokohama I came across a shark
who had the sort of cut and thrust for showbiz
   life
but was more concerned with finding a wife.
I found a plaice with the most expressive face,
but when I tried to put words into her mouth,
she spat them out. I found an eel
whose personality was electric, but she was too
   much
of a shocker for me. I trembled every time I
   touched her.
I found a pike I liked immensely, but
he didn't like me, spat in my eyes each time
I tried to handle him. There was a ray who I
   could pass
the time of day with and a monkfish had
   possibilities
till I discovered he had taken a vow of silence.

Then right at the end of my search, when I
    thought
I'd be returning to puppets and dolls,
I found a fish that was perfect. But although I
    swam
with him, ocean after ocean, offered him money,
    fortune
and fame, his name in lights, a season in Vegas,
he stubbornly refused to be swayed.

People would have paid thousands for the
    illusion
of a talking fish. In a world where we celebrate
the sham and the fake, fish ventriloquism
could have been my big break.

Flash Fish

(Dingle Aquarium, Ireland)

For a fish, she's a Mercedes,
a fish that knows she's flash,
a fish that knows she's turning heads
when she makes the occasional dash,

slipping from rock to hidey-hole
at strike-of-lightning speed
in an effort to burn off calories
and hoping to succeed

in winning admiration
for her contours and her poise,
she's a fish that knows she's flash,
and so do all the boys.

You can see them looking on,
you can see how much they wish
that they meant something special
to this fish that's such a dish.

But she's far too hoity-toity
and scares them all away.
'Come back when you grow up,'
you can almost hear her say.

She's a dolphin wannabe herself,
unhappy with her lot,
she knows she really should be
something that she's not,

a model perhaps, or a film star
with millions in the bank,
not a fish who just exists
inside a grotty tank.

She hopes that maybe one day
some film director might see
the talent that she has
and what a catch she'd be.

There must be something better,
there's got to be, she's sure.
Someone once found Nemo,
so surely they'll find her!

Talking Turtle
(New England Aquarium, Boston)

Everyone who visits the Aquarium
remembers the Big Momma turtle,
her grace and her poise in the water
and the name she's been given, Myrtle.

And we watch her navigating
as she tours around her tank.
Perhaps she'd like a boyfriend,
some fella called Casey or Hank.

Or maybe she'd like to shop for clothes
at some downtown fashion boutique,
to search out something flimsy
in a shape that is quite unique.

Or perhaps she could rent out her shell
as an advertising space,
to be seen by millions of visitors
who'd all recognize her face.

And if only Myrtle could talk,
what stories she could tell.
How good it would be to talk turtle
as your hand caresses her shell.

But frivolous thoughts don't disturb her much,
for Myrtle is far too wise.
You could learn the ocean's secrets
from the wisdom you see in her eyes.

And sometimes she flings herself on to her
    back
and imagines she's far out at sea,
staring up at the roof space
to the place where the stars ought to be.

Jellies

(New England Aquarium, Boston)

You couldn't say, 'Have a heart,'
to a jelly,
because it has no heart.
You couldn't say, 'Use your brain,'
to a jelly,
because if surgeons searched for weeks
they wouldn't find one.
You couldn't say, 'Stand up straight,'
to a jelly,
because jellies are spineless wimps.
So how come if jellies are
heartless, brainless and boneless,
how come if jellies are mostly water,
the Medusa jelly, the moon jelly,
the egg-yolk jelly, the umbrella jelly
are taking over our oceans
and filling up our seas.
Before long the children of jellies
and the children's children of jellies
will hardly have room themselves.

The warning is certainly clear:
Beware of the jelly babies!

You Cannot Take a Lobster Through Security

Had no trouble with lobsters when travelling
    British Rail,
and no one said we couldn't take the ferry,
but the airport officials all told me with one
    voice,
'You cannot take a lobster through security.'

They asked all kinds of questions: 'Is it pink or is
    it red?
Is it peaceful, is it vicious, is it live or is it dead?'
But no one was prepared to waive the rules and
    give
permission for us both to go ahead.

But they took my little brother who was bawling
    constantly,
and they took our Great-aunt Mabel who was
    more than ninety-three,
and they took a sumo wrestler who was wider
    than a tree,
but they wouldn't take my lobster through
    security.

I explained how my lobster was no mean
   mobster,
how it wasn't some disguised terrorist,
but they said that rules were rules and my
   lobster had to stay
till they'd come across some suitable checklist.

They hadn't any plans for the kind of body scans
that would illuminate crustaceans
and besides it might be hiding some item that it
   shouldn't
or be the subject of some special travel ban.

But they took my little brother who was bawling
   constantly,
and they took our Great-aunt Mabel who was
   more than ninety-three,
and they took a sumo wrestler who was wider
   than a tree,
but they wouldn't take my lobster through
   security,
no, they wouldn't take my lobster through
   security.

(Someone did actually try to take a lobster through security at Guernsey airport. A goldfish, a briefcase filled with bricks, a chainsaw and a partially frozen turkey have also been confiscated from passengers' luggage at other airports. Thanks to Danielle for the story.)

51

Only a Wardrobe

In the end it was, unfortunately,
only a wardrobe,
although hopes had been raised
that it could have been
an alternative route to Narnia.
For one thing the wardrobe was old,
ancient in fact, woodwormed
and waiting, surely, for four children
to come adventuring.
It was spacious too, and there were coats
and empty hangers that clanged
as they pushed past them.
But for Sharon and Tracey, Gavin and
Isaac it was disappointing.
They'd hoped for snow, a few flakes
at least to show they were on the right track,
but they'd not even felt cold.
They'd tapped and pushed and stamped,
hoping to discover a secret spring,
a trapdoor, an entrance way,
but nothing happened, no exciting window
to another world.

The wardrobe was simply a hollow space
and they'd just have to face it, life was dull,
adventures only happened on the screen,
in books, to others – they weren't for them.
In the end it was only a wardrobe
and I'd be lying to you if I said they found
    Narnia,
or indeed if any of us has.
The best secrets stay hidden, hidden deep,
but there is, and must always be,
something to search for,
always that slim chance.

Who Are These They?

Who are these they
who keep on saying
the weather will be a washout,
the winter will be wild,
the summer will be wet,
the weekend will be a write-off?
Who are these they
who like to warn of freak events
and unpleasant threats,
who always seem to know
what's on its way,
what's happening next?
Tell me, who are these they
and how do we know
if what they say is true?
How come they see much more than us?
How come the future is clear to them,
these they who always know
what's a mystery to us?

If only I could find out
who they are,
they could maybe predict
all kinds of things,
like racing results
and lottery wins,
but I suspect that those who are they
are really me and you.
But how can me and you be they
and say the things that they all say,
and make such forecasts every day?
There's no way that we can be they,
but who they are, I still can't say!

This Stream

This little scritch-scratch of a stream
is usually quiet,
travels its way unnoticed,
unremarked,
by day or by dark
keeps itself to itself.

But when the rain came
torrenting down,
this little stream
was a silent child
who suddenly found a voice.

Its chatter grew to a shout.
Its slow meander
quickened its pace,
turned into a race
against itself.

Suddenly the stream
felt important,
suddenly it had power.
Its hour had come.

It had a chance
to change its course,
to force down
the sentried rows of nettles
lining its bank,
to overspill into fields,
to let loose
a whoosh of water:

Hey, river, you've never
seen me like this before.
If you can't hold me
we'll shape new lakes,
we'll make this valley
a different place,
for I was a trickle,
but now I'm a ROAR
and nothing, yes
nothing, will be the same
as before.

Explorers

Let's explore the great outdoors,
Dad said, and leave our home behind.
Outside there's a wonderful world
and who knows what we'll find.

Let's wander about on mountains,
let's sleep beside the sea,
let's disappear into deserts
and drift wherever we please.

Let's fish for tarpon off Florida
and watch the gulls screech by.
Let's trek between rainforest trees
where we'll barely glimpse the sky.

We'll carry our home on our backs,
we'll camp by rivers and streams.
By day we'll follow railroad tracks,
by night we'll follow our dreams.

And we won't take the easy option,
we'll laugh when the going gets hard.
But just for tonight, we'll both play safe
and camp in our backyard.

Choirs

I wish there was a choir
for children like me,
children who can't sing a note,
children who growl
like they've gargled with gravel,
children with gorilla voices
who hoot and howl
and find comfort in cacophony.

I wish there was a choir
for children like me,
who desperately want to join in,
who strain to reach the highest notes
with looks on their faces
like they're in pain,
with comic-strip voices
that crack the music teacher's spectacles,
that cause zigzag lines
to spread down windows,
that shatter vases,
that encourage every dog for miles around
to howl in admiration.

So why are there no choirs
for children like me,
with voices that are dire
but enthusiasm that is vast.

What joy we would bring to ourselves
when we sing,
what a confidence boost
to know that we too
could make music.

Ordinary Really!

Wouldn't it be a scream
to meet the Queen
in a burger bar,
to see her royal limousine
in the parking lot,
to discover how she likes
to go undercover
when she's in the mood
for junk food.
Just imagine her
travelling back from some function
and just past junction five
on the M3
she has a sudden craving
for burned meat,
tells her chauffeur to stop
at Fleet Services
where ignoring pleas
from the Duke
she says, 'Back in a mo,'
and off she scoots,
a pair of dark glasses
covering her eyes.
Till fronting the queue
at last, she asks
for burger and chips, twice,

then realizes her enthusiasm
was rash,
for Her Majesty, of course,
carries no cash.
So she whips off her glasses
and glares at the guy
behind the bar.
'Young man,' she says,
'Don't you know who I am?'
And the guy says,
'Yeah, some lady who can't pay,
so disappear, be on your way.'
Until someone helps her out:
'Allow me, Your Majesty.'
'One is most grateful,'
comes the reply,
then she picks up her food
and hurries outside,
with everyone thinking,
what a surprise
to find the Queen of England
buying some fries.

Ordinary really,
just like us,
perhaps next week
she'll be taking the bus!

Middle Names

Do you know your teacher's middle name?

Would it be one that they'd be
too embarrassed to reveal?

Maybe it's something potty like Dotty
or silly like Chantilly,
something divine like Columbine
or medicinal like Calomine,
something modern like Ikea
or historical like Boadicea.

Perhaps it's something seasonal
like Primrose,
or a name that gets up your nose
like Hyacinth.

Maybe it's American like Hank
or solid and British like Frank.
Maybe it's barbaric like Conan
or boy-bandish and poppy
like Ronan.

Perhaps it's old fashioned
like Dora and Nora,
or something buttery
like Flora.

Maybe it's expensive like Pearl
or with a country twang like Merle.
Is it something classy like Clancy
or fancy like Nancy,
something biblical like Zachariah,
Amos, Moses or Jeremiah?

Is it witchy like Winnie
or moany like Minnie,
sensible like Fred,
countrified like Ned?

Is it tragic like Romeo
or Italian like Antonio?

Is it Zebedee or Gertrude,
Marvin or Ermintrude?
Is it Cecil or Boris,
Marmaduke or Doris?

Now go spread rumours
all around school.
Your teachers have names
that just aren't cool.

It's sure to embarrass them!

Send a Cow to Africa

I found a cow in the field behind my house,
and as the farmer seemed to have lots of them
I thought, well surely he won't miss one.
So I took the cow to the Post Office.
'Send this cow to Africa,' I said.

The man behind the counter wasn't happy.
'You could have put a nappy on this cow
before you brought her here,' he said.

'And besides,' he continued, 'you can't
send a cow to Africa.'

'Why not?' I asked.

'Because it's noisy and it's messy
and it's likely to get stressy.'

'You just can't do it,
there'd be nothing for it to chew, it
would starve before it got there.
And besides, it would be smelly.'

'It'll be bored, and someone might
get gored. The horns are a problem,
you see. No matter which way it's wrapped
they'll still stick out.'

'But I need to send this cow,' I said.
'And I don't care how much it costs,
as long as I can fill in a form
for if it gets lost.'

'Listen,' the man said. 'There's no way
we can send this cow. Not now
or any other day.'

'That's OK,' I said. 'I understand.
I'll send a goat to India instead!'

Scarecrows

It's not the dark, or snakes, or spiders,
or someone kidnapping me.
When I think of what I'm scared of,
it's scarecrows that scare me.

Scarecrows make me shiver,
they give me dreams at night,
the kind of dreams that make me scream
while reaching for the light.

I hate their pumpkin heads,
I hate their stringy hair.
I hate the way their eyes lock mine
and give me that frozen stare.

Across the fields they beckon,
I just can't turn away.
It feels as if they've cast
a gloomy spell upon my day.

I'm freakish about clowns,
guys and snowmen too.
But scarecrows with their twisted grins
scare me through and through.

There's an army of them gathering
out beyond our gate.
Their eyes are grim and glacial,
their faces full of hate.

At night I hear them shuffling,
splashing through the stream,
tramping over the fields,
trampling through my dreams.

I know that very soon now,
once fields are filled with frost,
they'll call and I'll be taken
by this legion of the lost.

Rooftops

I'd love to be able to move
through a city
on rooftops,
to take leaps of faith
as I jump from one building
to the next,
to feel like a superhero
with zero
to frighten me.

How good it would be
to race across acres
of roof tiles,
to slink over skylights,
to leap wide canyons
of streets on the curve
of an arc.

Television crews
would assemble
with reporters gasping out
the news,
wondering who
this is,
this lone leaper
in the dark.

And me, not knowing
where I'm going,
keeping moving,

thinking, hoping
one day I'll meet
another like me
who scoots across
roofs,
checking each time
where he plants
his feet.

Street after street,
mile after mile,
we'd explore
the hidden places
only helicopter pilots
would have seen.

I'd love to be able to move
through a city
on rooftops.

Passing Through

I'm watching next door's cat
window-shopping our chicken run.
He's a cat with a tick list
checking that nothing's changed.
Same six hens,
still as mannequins,
six pairs of eyes
locked on him.
Round the side he finds
the same broom,
same old angle
against the wire,
Same rabbit shut away,
no catch here, no point
in sniffing the latch.
Gap in the hedge
still open, same jump
sees him through.
Next door's cat
briefly pauses,
looks back,
till satisfied all
is as it should be,
moves on.

Earwigging

Earwigs keep appearing in our house,
and me, because I killed lots of creatures
as a boy, I keep airlifting them out
into the garden.
Or maybe it's the same earwig
that keeps coming back,
or maybe a whole family of earwigs,
maybe we're under attack.
I'm puzzled why earwigs find our house
so exciting, so enticing.
Maybe the news outside in the alley
is of some convention.
Maybe they've heard of some new invention
for making an earwig's life easier.

Maybe we could find out for sure
if only we could earwig earwigs!

Lost Albatross

In the bird world you're surely a jumbo jet,
but some failure in satnav must have upset
your coordinations and somehow you flew
thousands of miles from the places you knew,
till a glimpse of mountains and ice-carved rocks,
of dense pine forests and deep dark lochs
drew you down for a closer view
and you thought to yourself that this land would
    do.

Far away from the southern ocean,
the ebb and flow of the waves in motion,
the heave and swell of the storm's commotion.

And I really do feel such a sense of loss
for this sad and friendless albatross.
Forty years spent in such a lonely state,
forty years spent searching for a mate,
someone who'd make his heart beat faster,
help him forget his navigational disaster,
after wild winds blew him way off course
and he set up home in the heather and gorse.

Far away from the southern ocean,
the ebb and flow of the waves in motion,
the heave and swell of the storm's commotion.

And the bagpipes play their saddest lament
for this lost albatross's predicament.

Grey Day

It's a grey day today.
    The clouds are grey,
    the sea is grey,
    the grass is grey-
    ish . . .
I don't know who invented grey,
    but I hope it goes away
    and doesn't stay.
I don't want a grey day,
    I want a pink day
    or a yellow day,
    any kind of day
    except grey.
Wouldn't it be great
to take a brush and paint the sky
    purple or green.
We need something to brighten
    this grey day,
something to rip a hole in the sky
and let other colours slip through.
    A stream of pink,
    a waterfall of purple,
    green ink.

Where are the artists
    to work their magic
    on such a grey day?
Where are the wallpaper designers
    who'll cover the day
    with stripes or flowers?
Where are the fashion designers
    to dress the day
    in outrageous colours,
    or drape it with curtains,
    certain then to lose the grey,
    chase it away
    till tomorrow.

Going South

Word gets round
by word of mouth
or word of beak,
'We're going south.'

And everyone gathers
on telephone wires,
on tops of trees
on roofs or church spires.

No security checks,
no passport, no cases.
No border controls
closing off places.

The skies are ours,
we go where we please,
away from the damp
and the winter freeze.

And even though
they've only just come,
a party of swifts
on runway number one

are given priority,
so everyone waits
while there's last minute preening
or chatting with mates

till the skyway clears
and it's time to go.
'See you in Spain.'
'Meet you in Rio.'

We went there last year,
we know where we're going,
stretch out, lift off,
feel the air flowing.

Over the mountains,
the buildings and trees,
we're going south
on the pull of the breeze.

Ghosts of the London Underground

In the subway tunnels
   dying to be found,
on the Circle Line
   going round and round,
in the wail of the wind,
   a peculiar sound,
these ghosts
   of the London Underground.

Down, deep down, down deep underground
these ghosts of the London Underground.

And maybe you'll find
   you can see right through
the passenger sitting
   opposite you
or a skull appears
   from beneath a hood.
and you really wish
   you were made of wood,
that you didn't see
   what you think you did
and all these horrors
   were still well hid.

Down, deep down, down deep underground
with ghosts of the London Underground.

No ticket needed,
    you travel free
in the freakiest, scariest
    company.

Stand clear of the doors,
    we're about to depart,
so block up your ears
    and hope that your heart
is strong enough
    to survive the ride,
we're taking a trip
    to the other side.

Down, deep down, down deep underground
with ghosts of the London Underground.

And the tunnels echo
    with demonic screams
that chill your blood
    and drill into your dreams.
And you can imagine
    only too well
how these tunnels might lead you
    STRAIGHT INTO HELL . . .

Down, deep down, down deep underground
Down, deep down, down deep underground
Down, deep down, down deep underground
these ghosts of the London Underground.

these ghosts . . .

these ghosts . . .

these ghosts . . .

Omens

I saw the wild garlic flattened.
I saw the rain-drenched bee.
I saw the flecks of violet
in a bent wisteria tree.

I heard the babble of rooks.
I heard the startled horse.
I heard the river whisper
as the rocks broke up its force.

And I knew, for sure, that this year
summer would be short.

The Friendship Bench

Every colour
   and every creed,
people with money
   and people in need.
We want
everyone sitting on the friendship bench.

Football fans
   from rival teams.
'Beat you next time.'
   'In your dreams.'

We want Mums and Dads
   who can't get along,
brothers and sisters
   always in the wrong.
We want
everyone sitting on the friendship bench.

We want families crying,
   squabbling, bickering,
noisy neighbours'
   tempers quickening.

Overloud voices
    sounding out,
pressure groups shouting
    what they're about,
everyone sitting on the friendship bench.

We want criminals, judges,
    prisoners and jailers,
bullies and victims,
    thieves, blackmailers,
everyone sitting on the friendship bench.

No need to argue,
    no need to fight,
nobody thinking that
    might is right,
just
everyone sitting on the friendship bench.

We want positive, negative,
    black and white,
darkness giving way
    to the light.

We want hope for the future,
    lessons from the past,
the sort of friendship
    that lasts and lasts.
We want
everyone sitting on the friendship bench.

We want aggravation,
    assimilation,
recrimination,
    United Nations,
everyone sitting on the friendship bench.

From the naughty corner
    to the friendship bench,

everyone sitting on the friendship bench,
everyone sitting on the friendship bench,
everyone sitting on the friendship bench.

So go on, say who
    you'd like to see
on the friendship bench,
    sitting peacefully
with you
and
me.

Playing Safe

I've never felt the need
to test myself against fate
by riding the Wall of Death
or jumping eleven buses.

I've never felt the need
to bungee jump or free-fall
from a plane,
or run with bulls in Pamplona
or fight them elsewhere in Spain.

I've wondered sometimes
what it would be like
to bring more excitement
into my life.

And just occasionally I'll test myself,
jumping a ditch at
its not quite narrowest point,
walking a plank between two banks
or risking a peck from
a broody hen.

And then these little hints of danger
remind me how good it is
to play safe with my life.

Time

Time is like a thread that unwinds through our
    lives,
tight here, a bit of slack there.
Some people say they have too much time,
and that time hangs heavy.
I wish I could take some of theirs,
I never have enough time.
It would be great too if I could summon up time
from some time in the future,
grab a bit from when I'm older,
cut it out and say, 'Look, I'll have it now,
I can use it, I've got plenty to do with it.'
Or wouldn't it be great to have a computer bank
of stored time, a nationwide time bank
you'd just need a PIN to access,
to pay in or take out of . . .
Today's boring so I'd like to pay in three hours,
take it out again at the weekend
to stretch a day at Alton Towers.
That's how I felt when I was a child.
But now I'm older I think I might regret
all that time I took so eagerly,
spending it recklessly, wastefully,
letting it slip through my fingers,
thinking it was only time,
that there would always be plenty more,
but there's not . . .

Almost New Year

It's the last afternoon
of the old year
and already a full fat moon
is in charge of the sky.
It has nudged the sun
into a distant lake
and left it to drown,
while bare-branch trees
like blackened fireworks
burst with sunset.
Frost is patterning the fields,
a tractor tries to furrow
the iron-hard hill.
Winter's frown settles
on the face of the landscape.
It shrugs its shoulders,
gives in to January.

New Road

(*As Joni once wrote in one of her songs:*
'You don't know what you've got till it's gone.'*)

My ears are closed to the storm,
its voice no longer thunders.

The stream does not share its secrets.

I hear the rain's Morse code
on my roof,
but its message remains a mystery.

I no longer receive communications
on the breeze.

And trees have fallen silent,
their leaves done with whispering.

Birds and bees have nothing
to say to me.

For the road that's planned
through the valley
grows nearer
every day.

And everything turns its face away
as I walk by.

(*from 'Big Yellow Taxi' by Joni Mitchell)

Calling Your Name

('I call your name / but it becomes the wind.'*)

I remember quiet days when speaking your
   name
was a waft of air that we barely noticed.

I remember playful days
when my voice skipped with the breeze
then ran
between the trees, the dark forests,
over the cliffs and out to sea.

I remember solemn days when my voice
was a sheet that flapped on a line,
then filled with wind
and gusted.

And then one day, one sad day,
my voice became a hurricane
and blew you away.

(*from *'Pieces'* by *Tired Pony*)

Elvis RIP

'Elvis is dead,'
they said.
Lived life in
the fast lane,
then met with
something faster.

Too many late nights,
birds, the rat pack,
stalking women,
reactions must have
slowed.

We didn't see, of course,
and what you don't see
you don't always
believe.

Our dog too
refuses to believe.
Sees him everywhere,
gets spooked
by his ghost.

'Elvis is dead,'
they said.

But on moon-drenched nights
we wake sometimes
knowing he's out there.

Spotlit once more
and jailhouse rocking
our garden fence.